This Book Belongs to

_____

Parents:
Teach your children to pray
and encourage them everyday

A Child's Prayer

By Barbara Williford

GPublishing, LLC

Illustrator: SOS Graphics and Designs

Cover Design: SOS Graphics and Designs

Copy editor: Francene Ambrose Gunn

Publisher: G Publishing LLC
                  Detroit, Michigan

 ISBN 13: 978-0-9796978-7-6
          10: 0-9796978-7-5

Published and Printed in the United States of America

In the morning when I rise.

I see the sunshine.

I thank Jesus
for this day.

I pray for my dad.

I pray for my mom.

I pray for Sam, my pet dog.

And I pray for Sweety, my pet bird.

I pray for all the sick people.

I pray for my teacher.

But most of all, I pray for me.

Additional Books by Barbara Williford

Hope
Prayers that Exalt
He is Coming
The Traveler
The Sword
I Am God
God's Healing Power

Upcoming Children's Books

Praise the Lord
David the King

Printed in the United States
104455LV00001B

9780979697876